BAR NAPKIN LOVE LETTERS

Bar Napkin Love Letters

Blurred Lines from Dead Society Poet

JR Hataway

CONTENTS

As always, for Rae
The girl with sunrise in her eyes

FICTION OF MY PEN

I know the sound
all too well
words on repeat
north of the heart
in the sweet desperate hours
between now and then
angels and demons jockey for position
burning the truth
in the fiction of my pen
a story that needs telling
but much too heavy to leave the page

WANNABE BARD

I deal scattered tales of love and regret
hearts aflame and mythology of sunset
numberless souls and pyres yet to light
dancing whiskey tongues at broken midnight
songs of wishes cast at runaway stars
howls for the moon, fireflies in jars
I'm just a devil in the rain with no Jesus at the wheel
so loan me some ink and fire to steal
dreams of yesterday leave tomorrow scarred
but take no pity on this wannabe bard
this fool's narrative unwritten
would be such a crime
so sit down here and I'll spin you the truth...
one lie at a time

photo: Cottonbro Studio

RANSOM NOTES

We cast our net into the night
chasing memories
heavier than the sunsets
of where we once played
now imaginary friends
wield faulty weapons
parlor tricks of darkness and light
dancing ghosts
behind melancholy's veil
I burn ransom notes
from a misspent youth
writing poetry from what I remember

BORROWED SONG

Suzanne D. Williams

I wait on time
to loan me words
poetry is a patchwork
from fragments of my age
wetting asphalt
a thimble at a time
because I miss the smell of rain
I turn up my collar
when the wind stands rough
let love dance
my blood to flame
and warm these cold bones
steal me some magic
from the moon before I drown
and like the mockingbird
I'll sing you a borrowed song

DESOLATE DANCE

Memories flutter on sullen wings
at the windows of my mind
their rent is due
a desolate dance
once the lights fade
countless poems, untitled
recount conversations
with voiceless stars
and the moon
scolding me to grow up
they must serve
as my gift to you
they're all I can afford

THE ORDER OF THINGS

Let me hide from the wind
so I can spin you a tale
words freeze in this air
colder than the stone
that sharpens my axe
I've felled a grove
to kindle a song of fire
so dance with me
through the order of things
ignoring the ghosts
so we can love, laugh, and die

DECODE THE MYSTERY

Left to decode the mystery
of yesterday's dream
daggered by words
in books best left unread
forgetting is a freedom
that never calls my name
instead, a chorus of regret
moves the day
I cleave myself from those chains
just to fasten them around my neck
hoping no one will notice

REASON'S RULE

I listen to the sea
and its whiskey dusk whisper
I'd catch the wind if I could fly
jealousy floats easily to my tongue
instead, I stand my ground
clinching fists of nothing
like a frozen rose in fire
waiting to wilt
love is a risk worth taking
for a rebel to reason's rule

EPITAPHS OF POETRY

Anna-Louise

I recite for you
the words I learned
in my attempts
to mend the broken
shards of the former
consumed within
where fires rage
moving at a glacial pace
I dance through
my graveyard of memories
writing epitaphs of poetry
in the ashes

THINKING ABOUT THINKING

I took your dare
venturing forth
to kiss the stars
where angels buzz
and fly like music
tormenting flashes
in the heyday of my eyes
angry winds blow parallel
to my lying down bed
here I remain
anchored by my own chains
thinking about thinking
and wishing your constellation
was painted on my ceiling

FORGOTTEN GODS

A dance in silver light
I owe the winter moon
spellbound at midnight
seems brighter than noon
Northern lights on the wind
and stars in your hair
promiscuous blend
this honeyed poison we share
a devil's game we play
your wild heart, this poetic fool
the hidden bell tolls the day
as forgotten gods no longer rule

NO LESS TO CRAVE

I come from the sea
far away from the meadows
disarranged
in commotion of broken wings
outside of this love
tripping over my words
but still spilling truth
as time goes by
poisoning the memory
still I've no less to crave
as skeletons pound
the closet door
I can ruin it all
and still love you

MEANT FOR THE WIND

Creeping winter
breaks its silence
a chill unheard
sows discontent
in my bones
I steal some fire
and dance with embers
through the cutting garden
to harp on things dead to me
staking my claim to solace
with torn remnants of poetry
meant for the wind

Photo: Brigitte Tohm

YOUR CHAOS AND MINE

We dance amid talking walls
this song of the wild ones
tearing the roof off
as we laugh time away
bathed in savage rain
lightning glints on angel hair
poetry bleeds
from a tormented tongue
behind a rose in my teeth
with any luck
your chaos and mine
will outdare the night

THE COLOR OF FIRE

Laney-Jade Mondou

Taunting the grave
with a life yet unspent
we with crying hands
belong to the haunted
misfits on the ground
professing our love
to water and stars
where we dance like shadows
to songs of many shades
painting our midnight
the color of fire

JUDGE ME IN LOVE

I stop the world
to shatter this
pristine loneliness
bluebird song memories
return at wild horse gallop
flailing away at old bonds
swallowing the aurora
its amber fire halo
in mists of the moon
you might say I'm coloring
outside of the truth
judge me in love
if you must

WEARY DANCER

A weary dancer I've become
to time's tune of forgotten origin
I bleed ghosts from my pen
and lace my midnight
with forgotten angels
let the moon draw her blade
to sever the cord of dark existence
the lying mirror holds a stranger
that can't possibly be me

VOICES OF THE DEAD

Take me down
lure me to dream
sing to me your song of thunder
shake this glass house
with secret sins
and names never spoken
clasp the fury
of this beautiful lonely
as wine spills from trembling cups
until my verses inherit
voices of the dead

POCKETS OF MY SOUL

My words reclaim me
to fill this hollow room
voices in the mirror
strike the bell of liberation
trembling hands
burn another memory
no stranger to catastrophe
I dance in the flames
bending with the smoke
like starlings in murmuration
singing your name in the
pockets of my soul

UNPLANTED GHOST

Dawn sky swallows shadows
setting the stage
its labyrinthine muse
on full display
words fade in the hush of distance
and wind turns cold
on this unplanted ghost
salt no longer stings my wounds
as the dancing sea grows weary
of licking the shore
its forget-me-nots carved in stone

FROZEN FIRE

Subdued, I stand
staked to the hill
on which I will die
burning alive
in her poetry of frozen fire
as she tattoos her laughter
onto my soul

SNEAK AWAY

Sneak away from here
with me
we'll pick the locks
that hold the stars
and find all the ways
poetry is made

Photo: Alberlan Barros

EAGER TO RAGE

Standing my ground
sinking my toes into
what I thought I knew
my nightlong eyes
watch the moon
eager to rage
in her desolate kiss
setting fire to words written
in the alphabet of the wind
cumbersome in my attempts
to corral this love
that roars on its chain

ONE MORE FOR THE ROAD

Behind these scars
ghosts still drive me
push and pull
of a twofold entity
in balanced disarray
lullabies of silent screams
scatter like flaming doves
into poetry of my darkest secrets
so serve me up
one more for the road
and let me rage
as both whiskey and words
are burning my throat

TIME HAS NO NAME

Closing my eyes
on what's to come
I paint you pictures
with loaded words
you can't rush sunrise
when time has no name
searching for grace in hellfire
and madness in the wind
I dance my blood to flame
and bury my love
in letters to the moon

ZERO-SUM GAME

Raked pale by anger inside
my wasted words
roll off a mad tongue
just to burn in moonlight
night grinds away
to malefic melodies
between the shadows and me
a wounded poet
has no faith
in hidden gods
let the ghosts
collect my bones
and settle the score
in this zero-sum game

SEA OF POETRY

Cut me down
from these marionette strings
in this sideshow act
where reason wears
the darkest name
and reality scatters
like mad birds
chasing storms
I trace fractal patterns
of night and fury
drawing constellations
in your domain
just let me float away
on a sea of poetry
and I'll willingly drown
for you

POETIC MASQUERADE

A slave to vanity is the hand that rules
a burden clothed in misty agony
my naked heart fights for air
kin to sorrow
estranged from forgotten joys
a dance for a dime
in this poetic masquerade
where I burn for you in silence
holding my own feet to the fire

SHATTERED THINGS

I dance along a tightrope
writing poetry of shattered things
stolen kisses from the devil
fallen stars, broken rings
filling this dead space
with echoes of your name
as time wages war behind
a paper-thin smile of shame

Photo: Thiago Matos

TOMORROW'S SCREAM

Confined to a feeling
my poetic soul walks on fire
drawing wordy shapes in the ashes
a blind archer with arrow nocked
in the galloping night
taking aim at quiet dignity
faith drips from errant wounds
as today's blue hours
devolve into tomorrow's scream

COLORS OF YOUR WORLD

My voice drowns in the whispering wood
where blood moon shadows lick the ground
I sing of daydreams in dissonant melody
as lost wishes are wrung
from my grumbling hand
another cold hard lesson freezes my eyes
you'll find me here
scattered in the wind
where love wheels with the stars
and your sweet fire
stitches my broken halves
back together
in colors of your world

BANDIT GHOSTS

A guilty rain falls
and bleeds the fight
from my bones
a poetry formless
truer than the pain
leaving me to
burst at the seams
in its unsubtle crush
bandit ghosts
mistake my silence
for concession
it's just that I've
forgotten their names

MY DIE IS CAST

With a pocket full of dreams
all I know stirs in the gray
watching the world
through dusty windows
threadbare spines adorn this broken room
my die is cast midway to nowhere
there's no voice of reason
in my poetic downfall
where a moonblind soul
swings from oblivion's rope

PYRE OF MY SINS

Trade me a memory
to fill this empty dream
I lean on poetry
to bail me out again
lighting a pyre of my sins
piercing the tight aroma
of still night air
frail deeds steal my peace
in another empty field
where lonely stars still shine
but the stones are hostile
under my feet

LONG ARE THE DAYS

Long are the days
when buried thoughts bloom
nameless in the hours
writing out the dark
winded by insomniac storms
sewing a shroud of smoke
and gas station bourbon
ghosts of broken midnight
wield hammers of truth
and tears never cried
leave me cracked in the glory
like a saint about to fall

BURIED IN THE MEADOW

I drag out darkness
to sighs of a blood moon
ache drowns me in the night
swimming in layers
of collected thoughts
blowing off dust to remember
painting pictures
of shifting reflections
borrowing colors
from autumn leaves
reclaiming the land
that holds my oath
buried in the meadow
where we danced

Photo: Elias Tigiser

WHISKEY CHAINS

We lean into the night
longing between verses
hiding stars from the sky
the mad moon traverses
picking our tangled poison
to dance in whiskey chains
bellowing thunder
through rings of fire
no longer to dream in vain

BLUE NOTES OF THE MOON

Verses I bleed bring no peace tonight
winter wind spins the sky
its whispered nuance deafening
my blade falls dully
on tethers that moor my ghosts
give me the strength
to put these worries on ice
though I shiver to the kiss of time
my misfit heart doles out the rhythm
and blue notes of the moon
will sing me to sleep

POETRY'S LOST & FOUND

Shuttered heart frowns in winter blues
a wounded existence finds no glory in regret
when even saints fear the swinging bridge
my father's ghost
holds me hostage to a bloodline
stars fall cold
as I rage at the harbor's buoy bell
my oath long ago carved
into corroded steel
in poetry's lost and found

SEAFARER'S FABLE

Pixabay

Coming undone
but still holding my breath
I've no gold
for the fortune teller
praying you'll hear
my spoken word serenade
you wear the night
like a favorite satin gown
with a mystery that speaks
my native tongue
frantically I fall
to verses unwritten
as the sky runs out of moon
and I'm cast away
in a seafarer's fable

BEGGING FOR RAIN

Night sky pitches the moon
until dawn's trembling sun
thumps the clouds
to thin the veil
poetic inscriptions
written in ashes and dust
a graveyard of secrets at our feet
envious tongues
high and dry
sing an encore
of milk and honey
like muddy wildflowers
still begging for rain

DWELLING IN SILENCE

To my own devices
leave me
I hold down the fort
a painted false face
of dwelling in silence
between whispers, roars
and shots in the wind
eunuch battles rage
behind these walls
you'll never hear me
shout down every ghost
drowning each fear
just to sell you poetry
of inherited truths

MARTYR'S ODE

Sandbag the door until it's safe
yesterday's murmurs
bloom as ghosts on the edge
of another sleepless night
spilling words inside
my riddled stronghold
with heart nor head fit to lead
I spiral in flames of unvoiced love
a martyr's ode
written out of spite
carved into my bones

GULF OF LOATHING

With anchored tongue
I wield this pen in fury
a scythe harvesting memories
blown by broken winds
of a reluctant sunrise
marooned in a gulf of loathing
bound in the moon's dark allure
and the noose I tied myself
captive to the burn
the way heaven always
has a crush on hell

THE DWINDLING RIVER

Sins confessed by a nameless tongue
along the shoals of the dwindling river
ancient stories carved in the rocks
plagiarized by the poet
now left to pray to a darkening sky
lay down the law
and dress me in bittersweet redemption
camouflaged in the sting of the rain

THE WORLD I BREATHE

Artificial light and pumpkin spice
do not lessen the sting
of the world I breathe
hybrid emotions consume this empty space
torn to the core
I warm my bones
in fires of unfinished poems
and dance with smoky ghosts
to the melody of an alabaster half moon

SANDCASTLES

The loneliest road led me to the edge
of this beckoning sea
rushing in, a foolish notion,
to liberate my soul on the other side
or marinade in the regret
that sleeps in its depths and burns my lungs
maybe next time I'll be satisfied
with these castles built in the sand

Photo: Tomas Williams

POETRY'S WILDFIRE

Bathed in shadow
flirting with the sky
we dance along the night's dark edges
and look for Jupiter's face among the stars
maybe the moon can bless these tired wings
smoke in the meadow burns our eyes
and scratches laughter from our lungs
as poetry's wildfire is reborn

HANDS OF CLAY

Autumn's leaves pound
the surface of the world
drumming for a poet
lost in time's dance
at the edge of an hourglass
sinking further
into vermilion hues
a thousand kisses
of unseasonal colors
sing your praises
damn these hands of clay
hopelessly molding words
into the shape of you

STARS IN MY COUNTING

My poet's mind
cursed to overthink
doubt creeps like the mousing cat
I stuff my wounds
with colors of the night
and if the moon
declines my invitation
stars in my counting
will sate my eyes with love
just the same

Photo: Jayalekshman SJ

WRECKED ANGEL'S TEARS

Chained to a dream between
peace and pandemonium
struck senseless by the
cruel weight of winter
heel to toe on a knife's edge
turbulent and tender
naked as the trees
I fall with the stars
to a wrecked angel's tears
searching every bent possibility
for love to bless the dark

MY MORTAL GHOST

A heavy anger hammers my temples
stealing my breath when I come up for air
bending thoughts into digestible shapes
stirring up thunder to robe my mortal ghost
jealousy gets the best of me
when the moon dips her chaos in silence
proving once again
I have so much to learn

I CHASE EVERY STORM

I chase every storm
a poet's heart to blame
just to dance to thunder
when the rain calls your name

SAVE ME FROM ME

Unriddle my genesis
save me from me
and this urge within
to get in my own way
a frightened heart
speaking love letters
behind a sorrowful mask
empty as the wind
blowing through me
tearing at the seams
until I've no more cards
up my sleeve

THE BLIND SING SWEETER

Lost my eyes on the edge of never
so delightfully deceiving
vampires wind the clock
and tie the hands of time
resurrecting dark feelings
dressed in pretty words
far be it from me
to break with tradition
this weary heart
slips into fantasy again
I guess it's true that
the blind sing sweeter

Photo: Jon Tyson

SHADY GODS

Hear my voice
its shadow of a sound
though I swing regret by the tail
still life has muted my bones
stripped of skin
a barren self image
mirror to the shatter
anxiously awaiting
the next whim of shady gods

TRUTH FALLS SHORT

You became my poetry
in the weightless freedom
of dreams masquerading as reality
savoring stolen kisses
along curves of grace
intimate silks unfurl
to a lost soul in the hands of wonder
now flooding emotions
in a passionate haze
breach the dam in my pen
cold hard truths fall short
to somehow ice this ache
amid the inferno

KISS THE DEVIL

In static darkness unfolding
knocked arrows wait
to cleave my soul
pour me another
round of broken dreams
I'll kiss the devil
and carve forget-me-nots
into my own chalky tombstone
releasing my final words
as I whisper your name
through the narrow infinity

RESTLESS LOVE

I bring to you this restless love
headlong in the wind
through insomniac storms
hanging hope on the moon's touch
blank pages and unfinished poems
fill a heart-shaped void
fighting gravity
out here in the dark
where only your kiss
can break the chill
of these fevered dreams

HOMELESS GHOST

I call your name
in the spinning wind
where we danced
beneath the moon's tilted arc
she imparts her wisdom
carved in stone
upon our jagged love
written in the sand
harping on the tide
under gossiping stars
a homeless ghost, I wander
every time you kill me
with goodbye

POUR ME A FRIEND

I retreat into myself when evening comes
as the dying day turns a cold shoulder
I pour me a friend to illuminate the night
basking in the burn of love's mounting fire
and poetry's whiskeyed words
I dance on eggshells
to the drumbeat of a coming storm

ACHING WINGS

Alone in city sounds
the moon lost in numbing light
I tumble with the leaves
through this labyrinth
of dead-end avenues
vices and bent possibilities
deal their ultimatums
leaving too many reasons
to curse my aching wings
prolonging my departure
for distant dreams
that dwell in the wilds

SHIPWRECKS

With pockets full of dreams
the poet's coat gets heavy
I deafly toil to bind this soul
to scattered lines that
wrap me in my own truth
my feet to fire, I turn a blind eye
to tides that never touch the shore
scavenging shipwrecks
in every place I've felt lonely

THE STRANGEST TRUTH

I ache to ride the phantom winds
It's been too long in one place
setting out on the way of the nameless
no one will know
chasing the smell of thunder
and sounds of glass
outrunning mercy in a story untold
and only remembered at night
help me dispel the myth
of these junkyard dreams
I find the strangest truth
lies in the real

BUTTERFLY OF MY DREAMS

Rueful bones blush
when she sings my name
separating me from my woes
butterfly of my dreams
rages in a raven's waltz
performing a symphony
of perfect midnight
stopping the world
in a storm of unmade prediction
as she teaches tornadoes how to dance

MYSTERIES TO DECODE

Lured to darkness
with mysteries to decode
love was free to burn
in our repose from light
far away are the meadows
where time shed its wings
we drank the wind like wine
and I held beauty by the handful
now loneliness beats at my window
as the moon and I place bets
on which stars are already dead

SCARS I SELF-INFLICT

Meet me at midnight
on that deserted shore
selfish of me I know
I'm bound by threads
that resonate in my heart
kin to the tide and
ghosts that dance on the waves
let your kisses devour me
in the patient light of the moon's eye
you'll find your name
amongst all the scars I self-inflict

ENVY FOR THE WOLF

I wander in poetry
through forgotten meadows
borrowing lyrics
from the river's monologue
viewing the world
through phantom eyes
afflicted with envy for the wolf
and his devotion to the moon
tear me out of this dream
while the night
still resides in my veins
I give justice to this love
with my own song of the wild
drawing out a fire for you
that could never be bound in skin

WHISPERED POETRY

Hidden from the moon
west of life's happenings
weeping with the hourglass
as wonder dies
draped in the blue
of vacant days
and empty doorways
where your silhouette swayed
I curse the wind
that rustles the pages
as the whiskey glass
warms my blood
whispered poetry
hits like thunder
when all my nights
wear your name

CREATURE IN MY BONES

Time's riddles lie seeded
in the furrows of the ocean
and the legend of the rose
both lending words
to the creature in my bones
obedient to my obligation
standing my ground
against the lightning
as the sand shifts
beneath my feet
leave me to the mercy
of the tides and a moon
that taught me to dream
eyes a century older
will greet the dawn

LOVE AND DEATH

Over we fall
fastened to a name
struck down by
something never known
unwitting casualties
of matches held to paper hearts
where dances in the ashes become
tantrums of ambient static
all we are, entwined,
in the common threads
of love and death
both having no country
and waiting for no one

BEAUTY IN THE DARK

What more can we ask of the song?
stumbling in time
to beauty in the dark
burning like bourbon's kiss at midnight
hooked on the words
bleeding melody in borrowed shadows
of the moon's pale fire
where the only witnesses
are the ghosts that shape the music

BAR NAPKIN LOVE LETTERS

I am a collection of blurred lines
between shadowed scraps of twilight
and bar napkin love letters
sins of an unquiet mind
become jagged wounds
against a crumbling backdrop
sore feet, standing idly by
spilling secrets to the sea
nothing left to do
but apologize for being me

Photo: Oleksandra Sorokina

ACKNOWLEDGEMENTS

I thank all of my family and friends for your continuous love and support. The last couple years have been a whirlwind and I am eternally grateful to you all.

Most importantly, I thank my lucky stars everyday for the love of my life, Rae. The girl with "sunrise in her eyes" has taught me that true love does exist and even chumps like me get lucky once in a while! I love you.

Until next time,
DSP